MW00636124

Still Before the Dawn

Inspired words for encouragement,
comfort, and strength

Blessings to you!

Jody Reichel

Jody Bennett Reichel

Illustrations by Lucy McTier

Lydia Inglett Ltd. Publishing
Award-winning publisher of elegant books

Scriptures quotations marked (NIV) are taken from the *Holy Bible, New International Version*®. NIV®. Copyright © 1973, 1978, 1984 by International Bible Society.

Scriptures marked (NASB) are taken from the *New American Standard Bible*®. NASB®. Copyright © 1960, 1962, 1968, 1971, 1972, 1973, 1975, 1977, 1995 by the Lockman Foundation.

Scriptures marked (NKJV) are taken from the *New King James Version*®. NKJV®. Copyright © 1979, 1980, 1982 by Thomas Nelson Inc.

Scriptures marked (ESV) are taken from the *English Standard Version*®. ESV®. Copyright © 2001 by Crossway, a publishing ministry of Good News Publishers.

Scriptures marked (KJV) are taken from the *King James Version*®. KJV®. Copyright

Scriptures quotations marked (RSV) are taken from the *Revised Standard Version*®. RSV®. Copyright © 1946, 1952, and 1971 by the Division of Christian Education of the National Council of the Churches of Christ in the United States of America. Used by permission. All rights reserved.

Images of the Harbour Town Lighthouse painted and reproduced with permission and thanks to Sea Pines.

Still Before the Dawn

Jody Bennett Reichel

ISBN: 978-1-938417-31-3

© Copyright 2016-2017 Jody Bennett Reichel, Text
© Copyright 2016-2017 Lucy McTier, Illustrations
© Copyright 2016-2017 Concept Lydia Inglett Publishing

To order additional books and join our community: www.starbooks.biz

Published by Lydia Inglett Ltd. Publishing
www.lydiainglett.com
www.starbooks.biz
301 Central Ave. #181
Hilton Head Island, SC 29926
info@starbooks.biz

All rights reserved. No portion of this book may be reproduced, stored in a retrieval system, or transmitted in any form, or by any means—mechanical, electronic, photocopying, recording, or otherwise—without prior written permission from the publisher, except as provided by United States of America copyright law. Printed in China.

To order more copies of this or any of our books, visit our online bookstore

www.STARBOOKS.biz
The place for beautiful, thoughtful gift books.

Lydia Inglett Ltd. Publishing
Award-winning publisher of elegant books

DEDICATION

In loving memory of my beautiful mama, Jann Bennett, who always helped me believe in myself. She was my lifelong source of inspiration and an example of faith and strength, even as she fought for her life with lung cancer. In the last few days of her life, she encouraged me to write my book.

ACKNOWLEDGMENTS

To Rob, my husband, best friend, and editor in chief—Thank you for encouraging me to write this book. It would not be possible without you.

To my children, Andrew, Morgan, Jeffrey, and John David—Thank you for being a great source of inspiration and for your continued love and support. I am honored to be your mom.

To my daddy, Larry Bennett—Thank you for being the best role model and for always challenging me to be my best at whatever I do.

To my family and friends—Thank you for cheering me along on this journey. And to those who shared their brokenness with me, thank you for your strength and trust.

To my publisher, Lydia—Thank you for listening to me and making my vision for this book become a reality.

And to my illustrator, Lucy, whose beautiful artwork graces these pages—Thank you for truly capturing my heart and soul.

Praise to the Lord for His inspiration!

Welcome

I woke up at 4 a.m. for the seventh day in a row, tossing and turning, unable to get back to sleep. It was undeniable that God was calling me to get up, so I sought the sanctuary of my screened porch. It was there that I fell to my knees and cried out to Him in prayer. My heart was burdened with so much: my brother-in-law had throat cancer, my mama was battling terminal illness, and all four children, ages 14-25, were facing their own intense challenges. I opened my journal and began to pour out my heart, filling many tear-stained pages. I soon realized the sun had come up, and God had soothed my troubled soul by giving me words of comfort in a rhyming prose. I knew this was from the Lord, as I don't write this way.

This dreaded 4 a.m. wake-up call soon became my sweet, anointed date with Jesus. God began to speak to me, not only in the wee hours, but also on my beach walks, bike rides, anywhere, anytime.

I started sharing my poems with those for whom I was praying. I prayed that the words He had given me could bless a wider audience. Amazingly, my poems were soon published with an inspirational greeting card company, my lyrics were sung by a well-known recording artist, and my framed writings were sold in stores.

Many years have passed since that early porch time with my Lord, but it is still my place of communion with Him. As I continued to seek God's purpose for my poems, He led me to compile my writings in this book.

My prayer for you is that as you stroll through these pages, you will find joy, encouragement, and peace in the sanctuary of your soul.

Hugs and Blessings,

Jody

"Praise be to the God and Father of our Lord Jesus Christ, the Father of compassion and the God of all comfort, who comforts us in all our troubles, so that we can comfort those in any trouble with the comfort we ourselves receive from God." II CORINTHIANS 1:3-4 NIV

JODY BENNETT REICHEL

Contents

Adversity

No one knows your troubled heart
Except the Lord Himself,
No matter what you're going through
He is there when you need help.

"Do not let your hearts be troubled. You believe in God; believe also in me."

JOHN 14:1 (NIV)

When the hard times come
God won't let you get crushed,
When you're anxious or worried
Don't despair, but simply trust.

When you feel overwhelmed
He won't abandon you,
Fix your eyes on Christ
And He'll help you through.

"The Lord also will be a refuge for the oppressed, a refuge in times of trouble."

PSALM 9:9 (KJV)

"We are hard pressed on every side, but not crushed; perplexed, but not in despair."

2 CORINTHIANS 4:8 (NKJV)

"Be of good courage, and He shall strengthen your heart, all ye that hope in the Lord."

PSALM 31:24 (KJV)

No matter how tough life is
There's nothing too hard for God,
His love is never shaken
Rest in His healing hand above.

"'Though the mountains be shaken and the hills be removed, yet My unfailing love for you will not be shaken, nor My covenant of peace be removed,' says the Lord, who has compassion on you."

ISAIAH 54:10 (NIV)

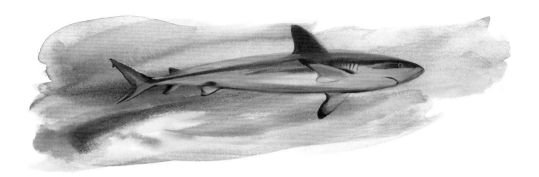

When deep waters of affliction
Start to flood over you,
He'll hear your plea for help
God's love will get you through.

"When you pass through the waters, I will be with you; and through the rivers, they will not overflow you. When you walk through the fire, you will not be scorched, nor will the flame burn you. 'For I am the Lord your God, The Holy One of Israel, your Savior.'"

ISAIAH 43:2-3 (NASB)

Anxiety

Focus on the present
The here and the now,
No worries for tomorrow
God will help you with His power.

"Cast your cares on the Lord and
he will sustain you; he will never
let the righteous be shaken."

PSALM 55:22 (NIV)

God is your refuge and strength
Trust Him for your cares each day,
Anxiety adds too much stress
Give it all to Him today.

"Trust in Him at all times, O
people; pour out your heart before
Him; God is a refuge for us."

PSALM 62:8 (NASB)

Comfort

Nothing can separate
You from God's love,
May He fill you with hope,
Peace, and joy from above.

"Now may the God of hope fill you
with all joy and peace in believing,
that you may abound in hope by
the power of the Holy Spirit."

ROMANS 15:13 (NKJV)

God is with you and for you
There is nothing you face alone,
So don't be anxious
He will carry you safely home.

"I am with you and will watch over you wherever you go, and I will bring you back to this land. I will not leave you until I have done what I have promised you."

GENESIS 28:15 (NIV)

When your days seem long
And your nights are dreary,
Wrap up in Christ's arms
He'll comfort the weary.

"He gives strength to the weary and increases the power of the weak."

ISAIAH 40:29 (NIV)

"But as for me, I shall sing of Your strength; yes, I shall joyfully sing of Your loving-kindness in the morning, for You have been my stronghold and a refuge in the day of my distress."

PSALM 59:16 (NASB)

Depression

One of the greatest dangers faced
Is the gloom of self-pity,
Fix your eyes on Christ alone
Who brings light to the needy.

"When I am afraid, I will trust in You."

PSALM 56:3 (NIV)

"Therefore, holy brothers and sisters, who share in the heavenly calling, fix your thoughts on Jesus, whom we acknowledge as our apostle and high priest."

HEBREWS 3:1 (NIV)

Encouragement

As the Master of the mind
And Healer of the heart,
With God's tenderness and love
He'll hold you close and never depart.

"The Lord your God in your midst, The Mighty One, will save; He will rejoice over you with gladness, He will quiet you with His love, He will rejoice over you with singing."

ZEPHANIAH 3:17 (NKJV)

Sometimes friends fail us
But there's One who never will,
He's our dear Heavenly Father
Who keeps us calm and always still.

"And the Lord, He is the One who goes before you. He will be with you, He will not leave you nor forsake you; do not fear nor be dismayed."

DEUTERONOMY 31:8 (NKJV)

Faith

**Through the power of faith
He'll equip you today,
Though you can't see or feel
God is leading the way.**

"And Jesus said to him, 'If you can! All things are possible to him who believes.'"

MARK 9:23 (RSV)

"Now faith is the assurance of things hoped for, the conviction of things not seen."

HEBREWS 11:1 (NASB)

Have faith!
Believe! Trust in Him.
God has the power
to help you win.

"He replied, 'Because you have so little faith. Truly I tell you, if you have faith as small as a mustard seed, you can say to this mountain, 'Move from here to there,' and it will move. Nothing will be impossible for you.'"

MATTHEW 17:20 (NIV)

"But he said to me, 'My grace is sufficient for you, for my power is made perfect in weakness.' Therefore I will boast all the more gladly about my weaknesses, so that Christ's power may rest on me."

2 CORINTHIANS 12:9 (NIV)

When the world seems dark
And you can't see out,
Trust and walk by faith
The Lord will help you get about.

"For we walk by faith, not by sight."

2 CORINTHIANS 5:7 (NASB)

Fear

Look ahead to God
Let go of all fear,
Even if you fall
Your Savior is near.

"The eternal God is your refuge, and underneath are
the everlasting arms; He will thrust out the enemy
from before you, and will say, 'Destroy!'"

DEUTERONOMY 33:27 (NKJV)

forgiveness

Through God's love He will chasten
Until you're in harmony with Him,
Your sins are covered and forgiven
By God's grace, you can start again.

"Blessed is he whose transgressions are forgiven, whose sins are covered. Blessed is the man whose sin the Lord does not count against him."

PSALM 32:1-2 (NIV)

Friendship

We all need each other
Friends to talk to and trust,
But first we need our Lord
Depending on Him is a must.

"But if we walk in the Light as He Himself is in the Light, we have fellowship with one another, and the blood of Jesus His Son cleanses us from all sin."

1 JOHN 1:7 (NASB)

With a love so deep
My heart can feel with you.
Let me hold your hand
With friends that stick like glue.

Our Lord will never let
You stand alone for long.
Forever He will comfort
Your spirit with a song.

As some days may seem dark,
Look in your garden with hope.
Your angel friends, like flowers,
Will bring peace and help you cope.

"For He will give His angels charge concerning you, to guard you in all your ways. They will bear you up in their hands, that you do not strike your foot against a stone."

PSALM 91:11-12 (NASB)

God's Love

He is a God of unchanging love
With endless power from above,
The same today and tomorrow, too
Jesus Christ is forever true.

"The Lord appeared to us in the past, saying: 'I have loved you with an everlasting love; I have drawn you with unfailing kindness.'"

JEREMIAH 31:3 (NIV)

"Jesus Christ is the same yesterday and today and forever."

HEBREWS 13:8 (NIV)

God loves you ...
Higher than the stars
Deeper than the sea,
He cares for your heart
More than you dare to dream.

God made you unique
With a purpose and a plan,
You are His masterpiece
Created by His hand.

"So that Christ may dwell in your hearts through faith. And I pray that you, being rooted and established in love, may have power, together with all the Lord's holy people, to grasp how wide and long and high and deep is the love of Christ."

EPHESIANS 3:17-18 (NIV)

Nothing can wash away
The strength of God's love,
It's the most powerful force
That is given from Above.

"Many waters cannot quench love, nor will rivers overflow it. If a man were to give all the riches of his house for love, it would be utterly despised."

SONG OF SOLOMON 8:7 (NASB)

"The Lord is my strength and my shield; my heart trusts in Him, and He helps me. My heart leaps for joy, and with my song I praise Him."

PSALM 28:7 (NIV)

Let the light of God's love
Shine faith in your heart,
As you embrace one another
Perfect joy He will impart.

"There is no fear in love; but perfect love casts out fear, because fear involves punishment, and the one who fears is not perfected in love."

1 JOHN 4:18 (NASB)

God's Presence

As God's presence shines through
Deep recesses of your soul,
I pray renewing for you
That your heart can be made whole.

"No man will be able to stand before
you all the days of your life. Just as I
have been with Moses, I will be with
you; I will not fail you or forsake you."

JOSHUA 1:5 (NASB)

As you seek the Lord each day
You'll find Him wherever you go,
He's in the sunlight and the rain
And in the deep valley below.

"Commit your way to the Lord; trust in him and he will do this: He will make your righteousness shine like the dawn, the justice of your cause like the noonday sun."

PSALM 37:5-6 (NIV)

"Seek the Lord and His strength; seek His face continually. Remember His wonders which He has done, His marvels and the judgments uttered by His mouth."

PSALM 105:4-5 (NASB)

Seek the Lord's face
Open your heart to His presence,
As His love pours in
There will be no distance.

"When You said, 'Seek My face,'
my heart said to You, 'Your face, O
Lord, I shall seek.'"

PSALM 27:8 (NASB)

Christ is always with you
Friend, companion everyday,
As God's child He will never leave
He'll carry you each step of the way.

"I am with you and will watch over you wherever you go, and I will bring you back to this land. I will not leave you until I have done what I have promised you."

GENESIS 28:15 (NIV)

God's Promise

Don't try to figure out
What tomorrow holds,
Cling to God's promises
And His peace you'll behold.

"Finally, brethren, whatever things
are true, whatever things are noble,
whatever things are just, whatever
things are pure, whatever things are
lovely, whatever things are of good
report, if there is any virtue and if
there is anything praiseworthy—
meditate on these things."

PHILIPPIANS 4:8 (NKJV)

Grief

As you deal with pain and grief
And walk along the path of woe,
You keep seeking relief
For you're at your all time low.

The Lord's there to hold you up
God will help you win the fight,
He will fill your empty cup
With His grace and realms of light.

"God is our refuge and strength, an ever-present help in trouble. Therefore we will not fear, though the earth give way and the mountains fall into the heart of the sea, though its waters roar and foam and the mountains quake with their surging."

PSALM 46:1-3 (NIV)

Guidance

When God shines His light
And then darkness falls,
Be still and quiet
Until you hear His call.

"For God, who said, 'Let light shine out of darkness,' made his light shine in our hearts to give us the light of the knowledge of God's glory displayed in the face of Christ. But we have this treasure in jars of clay to show that this all-surpassing power is from God and not from us."

2 CORINTHIANS 4:6-7 (NIV)

Don't race ahead of God
Give Him charge of your day,
Walk one step at a time
He'll show you the way.

"Therefore do not worry about tomorrow, for tomorrow will worry about its own things. Sufficient for the day is its own trouble."

MATHEW 6:34 (NKJV)

As you seek the Father
Listen to what He has to say,
As He fills you with His spirit
Giving you strength along the way.

"Show me Your ways, Lord, teach me your paths; guide me in Your truth and teach me, for You are God my Savior, and my hope is in You all day long."

PSALM 25:4-5 (NIV)

Sit still in God's presence, Let His love surround you,
As you give Him thanks, God's light will shine through.

"Therefore by Him let us continually offer the
sacrifice of praise to God, that is, the fruit of our
lips, giving thanks to His name."

HEBREWS 13:15 (NKJV)

Healing

I pray dear Jesus
You bring relief,
The touch of Your hand
Gives healing and peace.

"And the God of all grace, who called you to His eternal glory in Christ, after you have suffered a little while, will Himself restore you and make you strong, firm and steadfast."

1 PETER 5:10 (NIV)

"Heal me, Lord, and I will be healed; save me and I will be saved, for You are the one I praise."

JEREMIAH 17:14 (NIV)

God seeks the lost and lonely
And draws them to Himself,
He heals the weak and injured
There is no one else.

"He heals the brokenhearted and binds up their wounds."

PSALM 147:3 (NIV)

"I will search for the lost and bring back the strays. I will bind up the injured and strengthen the weak, but the sleek and the strong I will destroy. I will shepherd the flock with justice."

EZEKIEL 34:16 (NIV)

Heaven

Please celebrate today
The life God's given me,
Smile, laugh, and sing
Heaven's a better place to be.

"But our citizenship is in heaven. And we eagerly await a Savior from there, the Lord Jesus Christ."

PHILIPPIANS 3:20 (NIV)

Don't seek what is below
Only look to God above,
For this earth will pass away
What remains is His love.

Our trust should never be
In people or things we own,
For our hearts should always rest
In our Heavenly Father alone.

"For our light and momentary troubles are achieving for us an eternal glory that far outweighs them all. So we fix our eyes not on what is seen, but on what is unseen, since what is seen is temporary, but what is unseen is eternal."

2 CORINTHIANS 4:17-18 (NIV)

Hope

"And my God will supply all your needs according to His riches in glory in Christ Jesus."

PHILIPPIANS 4:19 (NASB)

It is hard to rise above
Hurt, pain, and needs,
Give it all up to Him
And He will help you believe.

"Be anxious for nothing, but in everything by prayer and supplication with thanksgiving let your requests be made known to God. And the peace of God, which surpasses all comprehension, will guard your hearts and your minds in Christ Jesus."

PHILIPPIANS 4:6-7 (NASB)

God is above all things
Your problems and your pain,
When you behold His face
Peace and strength you will gain.

"And God raised us up with Christ and seated us with him in the heavenly realms in Christ Jesus."

EPHESIANS 2:6 (NIV)

In moments of confusion
And times of despair,
Focus your mind on Christ
And He'll calm all your cares.

"For You have been my help, and in the shadow of Your wings I sing for joy. My soul clings to You; Your right hand upholds me."

PSALM 63:7-8 (NASB)

Whether in darkness or light
The Lord is with you each day,
His light will continually shine
And help show you the way.

"Even the darkness is not dark to You, and
the night is as bright as the day. Darkness
and light are alike to You."

PSALM 139:12 (NASB)

Hope is the golden cord
That connects you heaven bound,
It lifts your head up high
Where God's presence can be found.

"Rejoicing in hope, persevering in
tribulation, devoted to prayer,"

ROMANS 12:12 (NASB)

Joy

How do you find joy?
In the presence of your King.
Give it all up to Christ
Soon hope and peace He'll bring.

"For You, O Lord, have made me glad
by what You have done. I will sing for
joy at the works of Your hands."

PSALM 92:4 (NASB)

Singing God's Praise
At the start of the day,
Lifts the heart and soul
To help you rejoice on your way.

"Let us come before him with thanksgiving and extol Him with music and song."

PSALM 95:2 (NIV)

"This is the day the Lord has made; we will rejoice and be glad in it."

PSALM 118:24 (NKJV)

Loneliness

Dealing with pain in silence
Can make you feel alone,
Remember God is there
To carry you safely home.

"I waited patiently for the Lord; he turned to me and heard my cry. He lifted me out of the slimy pit, out of the mud and mire; he set my feet on a rock and gave me a firm place to stand. He put a new song in my mouth, a hymn of praise to our God. Many will see and fear the Lord and put their trust in him."

PSALM 40:1-3 (NIV)

When you feel so alone
It's not God who leaves,
Whisper Jesus' name
He'll quietly bring peace.

"Then you will call, and the Lord will answer; you will cry for help, and he will say: 'Here am I.'"

ISAIAH 58:9 (NIV)

"I am with you and will watch over you wherever you go, and I will bring you back to this land. I will not leave you until I have done what I have promised you."

GENESIS 28:15 (NIV)

Nothing can separate you, From God's loving grace, When you're lonely or sad, Look to the Lord and pray.

"For I am convinced that neither death, nor life, nor angels, nor principalities, nor things present, nor things to come, nor powers, nor height, nor depth, nor any other created thing, will be able to separate us from the love of God, which is in Christ Jesus our Lord."

ROMANS 8:38-39 (NASB)

Marriage

Like four legs on a table
With balance and rest,
So a marriage should be
When put to the test.

"That is why, for Christ's sake, I delight
in weaknesses, in insults, in hardships, in
persecutions, in difficulties. For when I
am weak, then I am strong."

2 CORINTHIANS 12:10 (NIV)

A marriage takes
Commitment and love,
Respect and forgiveness
Through our God above.

"The Lord has done this, and it
is marvelous in our eyes."

PSALM 118: 23 (NIV)

Obedience

Make me a help to the helpless
To show Christ in a special way,
Radiating His love to many
All throughout the day.

"Even as I try to please everyone in
every way. For I am not seeking my
own good but the good of many, so
that they may be saved."

1 CORINTHIANS 10:33 (NIV)

Let Christ be your center
He's all that you need,
Fix your eyes on Him
He'll help you to see.

"Jesus answered, 'I am the way and the truth and the life. No one comes to the Father except through me.'"

JOHN 14:6 (NIV)

Pain

Pour out your heart to Him
Your cry in pain is heard,
God is your refuge and strength
Finding comfort through His Word.

"Trust in him at all times, you people; pour out your hearts to him, for God is our refuge."

PSALM 62:8 (NIV)

Christ knows your heart
And feels your pain,
He'll meet your needs
Again and again.

"And my God will meet all your needs according to the riches of his glory in Christ Jesus."

PHILIPPIANS 4:19 (NIV)

"For he has not despised or scorned the suffering of the afflicted one; he has not hidden his face from him but has listened to his cry for help."

PSALM 22:24 (NIV)

Parenting

The prayer for our child
Is that they put God first,
And draw near to the Lord
Where they find their self-worth!

"Draw near to God and He will draw near to you. Cleanse your hands, you sinners; and purify your hearts, you double-minded."

JAMES 4:8 (NKJV)

"Show me Your ways, Lord, teach me your paths; guide me in your truth and teach me, for you are God my Savior, and my hope is in you all day long."

PSALM 25:4-5 (NIV)

Every breath a parent breathes
Every prayer a parent prays,
Is a heart that's overflowing
With God's love for their child each day.

"I will give thanks to You, O Lord
my God, with all my heart, And will
glorify Your name forever."

PSALM 86:12 (NASB)

We can't help wrong choices
That our children sometimes make,
God is holding you so close
He knows your heartache.

"Be strong and courageous. Do not be afraid or terrified because of them, for the Lord your God goes with you; he will never leave you nor forsake you."

DEUTERONOMY 31:6 (NIV)

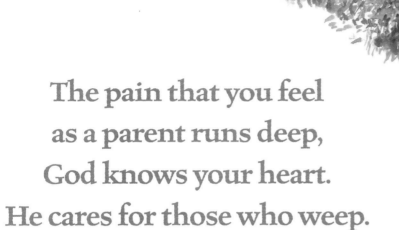

The pain that you feel
as a parent runs deep,
God knows your heart.
He cares for those who weep.

"Surely God is my help; the Lord is the
one who sustains me."

PSALM 54:4 (NIV)

"Praise be to the Lord, to God our Savior,
who daily bears our burdens."

PSALM 68:19 (NIV)

Peace

God is your answer
When questions worry your soul,
He is there to give peace
And His love makes you whole.

"Do not be anxious about anything, but in every situation, by prayer and petition, with thanksgiving, present your requests to God. And the peace of God, which transcends all understanding, will guard your hearts and your minds in Christ Jesus."

PHILIPPIANS 4:6-7 (NIV)

In the midst of a raging storm
And the force of a mighty wind,
God waves His hand over all
To allow calm in your life again.

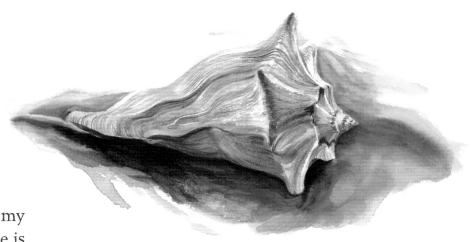

"Yes, my soul, find rest in God; my hope comes from him. Truly he is my rock and my salvation; he is my fortress, I will not be shaken."

PSALM 62:5-6 (NIV)

When life gets hectic
You're racing here and there,
Take time to rest
In God who cares.

As you get alone
And draw near to Him,
He'll renew your faith
From beginning to end.

"Above all, taking the shield of faith with which you will be able to quench all the fiery darts of the wicked one."

EPHESIANS 6:16 (NKJV)

As nature reveals calamity
And the storm rages on,
God promises to bring peace,
Tranquility, and calm.

"'Though the mountains be shaken and the hills be removed, yet my unfailing love for you will not be shaken nor my covenant of peace be removed,' says the Lord, who has compassion on you."

ISAIAH 54:10 (NIV)

Praise

The Lord is my Helper
He's my strength and my song,
With great adoration
I'll sing His praise all day long.

"Sing to him a new song; play
skillfully, and shout for joy."

PSALM 33:3 (NIV)

I will sing praise in the good
I'll thank God in the bad,
No matter the circumstance
Singing praises makes Him glad.

"In everything give thanks;
for this is the will of God in
Christ Jesus for you."

1 THESSALONIANS 5:18 (NKJV)

Give thanks to the Lord
Rejoice in your day,
As you focus on Him
He'll send blessings your way.

"This is the day the Lord has made;
We will rejoice and be glad in it."

PSALM 118:24 (NKJV)

"And my God shall supply all your
need according to His riches in
glory by Christ Jesus."

PHILIPPIANS 4:19 (NKJV)

Sing to God in the morning
Praise at the close of the day,
He will wash away your cares
And bring sunshine on your way.

"For his anger lasts only a moment,
but his favor lasts a lifetime;
weeping may stay for a night, but
rejoicing comes in the morning."

PSALM 30:5 (NIV)

Prayer

Prayer is such a treasure
As I can talk to God each day,
He listens to all my needs
Directs and shows me the way.

Prayer gives me peace and rest
It's what keeps me close to Him,
As I listen to my Father
He will guide each time again.

"And pray in the Spirit on all occasions with all kinds of prayers and requests. With this in mind, be alert and always keep on praying for all the Lord's people."

EPHESIANS 6:18 (NIV)

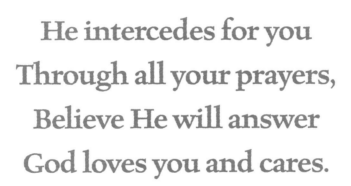

God is your helper
Who hears your heart,
Give it all to Him
He will never depart.

He intercedes for you
Through all your prayers,
Believe He will answer
God loves you and cares.

"Therefore, since we have a great high priest who has passed through the heavens, Jesus the Son of God, let us hold fast our confession. For we do not have a high priest who cannot sympathize with our weaknesses, but One who has been tempted in all things as we are, yet without sin. Therefore let us draw near with confidence to the throne of grace, so that we may receive mercy and find grace to help in time of need."

HEBREWS 4:14-16 (NASB)

Sometimes God calls you
To a quiet place of rest,
He surrounds you with love
So you can see His best.

"Then go inside and shut the door behind you
and your sons. Pour oil into all the jars, and as
each is filled, put it to one side."

2 KINGS 4:4 (NIV)

Be steady and at peace
Christ will meet all your needs,
With prayer and thanks to Him
He'll give grace so you can see.

"These things I have spoken to you, that in Me you
may have peace. In the world you will have tribulation;
but be of good cheer, I have overcome the world."

JOHN 16:33 (NKJV)

Protection

Guard your heart, soul, and mind
Against the evils of this world,
Say a prayer of thanks to God
Rest in His presence and His word.

"You are my hiding place; you will protect me from trouble and surround me with songs of deliverance."

PSALM 32:7 (NIV)

"How blessed are the people who know the joyful sound! O Lord, they walk in the light of Your countenance."

PSALM 89:15 (NASB)

When your life gets stirred up
You start to plummet to the ground,
God will catch you when you fall
Where His safety can be found.

"As an eagle stirs up its nest, hovers over its young, spreading out its wings, taking them up, carrying them on its wings."

DEUTERONOMY 32:11 (NKJV)

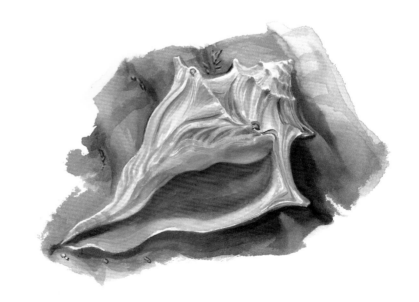

Renewal

Come to the Father
With an empty heart,
And open arms
For a brand new start.

"He gives power to the weak, and to those who have no might He increases strength. Even the youths shall faint and be weary, and the young men shall utterly fall, but those who wait on the Lord shall renew their strength; they shall mount up with wings like eagles, they shall run and not be weary, they shall walk and not faint."

ISAIAH 40:29-31 (NKJV)

God, take away my worries
Please remove all this pain,
Take me to a resting place
To see Your face again.

"He says, 'Be still, and know that I am God; I will be exalted among the nations, I will be exalted in the earth.'"

PSALM 46:10 (NIV)

Rest

When you feel exhausted
Cling to Christ even more,
Peace and rest He will give
Your strength He will restore.

"Trust in the Lord with all your heart and lean not on your own understanding; in all your ways submit to him, and he will make your paths straight."

PROVERBS 3:5-6 (NIV)

Rest and relax
Let your thoughts go,
Wait on His presence
His love you will know.

"Seek the Lord and His
strength; seek His face
continually."

PSALM 105:4 (NASB)

Strength

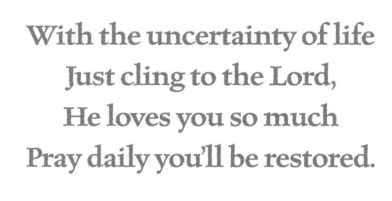

With the uncertainty of life
Just cling to the Lord,
He loves you so much
Pray daily you'll be restored.

"Surely God is my salvation; I will trust and not be afraid. The Lord, the Lord himself, is my strength and my defense; he has become my salvation."

ISAIAH 12:2(NIV)

When you wake up each day
Get dressed and prepare,
God will equip you with His armor
To fight the prince of the air.

"Put on the full armor of God, so that
you will be able to stand firm against
the schemes of the devil."

EPHESIANS 6:11 (NASB)

God …
You are my refuge,
You are my strength,
You're always there for me
You meet all my needs!

"With Your help I can advance against a troop; with my God I can scale a wall."

PSALM 18:29 (NIV)

"But as for me, I shall sing of Your strength; yes, I shall joyfully sing of Your loving-kindness in the morning. For You have been my stronghold and a refuge in the day of my distress."

PSALM 59:16 (NASB)

The enemy is out there
On the prowl, to devour,
Be alert and self-controlled
God will strengthen you every hour.

"Be of sober spirit, be on the alert. Your adversary, the devil, prowls around like a roaring lion, seeking someone to devour. But resist him, firm in your faith, knowing that the same experiences of suffering are being accomplished by your brethren who are in the world."

1 PETER 5:8-9 (NASB)

Be strong for today
God will meet your needs,
He'll empower you with strength
So you will always believe.

"And my God shall supply all your need according to His riches in glory by Christ Jesus."

PHILIPPIANS 4:19 (NKJV)

When the great storms of life
Bring trouble to your soul,
Reach out and grab God's hand
He'll give strength to make you whole.

"You have also given me the shield
of Your salvation; Your right hand
has held me up, Your gentleness
has made me great."

PSALM 18:35 (NKJV)

Stress

Quiet tension is not trust
It lessens your strength,
Give God your cares
Peace and power you'll receive.

"Cast all your anxiety on him
because he cares for you."

1 PETER 5:7 (NIV)

"Anxiety weighs down the heart,
but a kind word cheers it up."

PROVERBS 12:25 (NIV)

Surrender

Come to Christ
Relax in Him,
Live in His grace
And God's presence again.

"Be anxious for nothing, but in everything by prayer and supplication with thanksgiving let your requests be made known to God. And the peace of God, which surpasses all comprehension, will guard your hearts and your minds in Christ Jesus."

PHILIPPIANS 4:6-7 (NASB)

God has brought you this far
But He wants you all His own,
I'm praying and believing
That you will make your heart His home.

"Therefore, if anyone is in Christ, he is a new creation; old things have passed away; behold, all things have become new."

2 CORINTHIANS 5:17 (NKJV)

Thankfulness

Whatever you ask in God's name
Is heard by Him as you pray,
Thank your Father in advance
For His answered prayer this day.

"This is the confidence which we have before Him, that, if we ask anything according to His will, He hears us. And if we know that He hears us in whatever we ask, we know that we have the requests which we have asked from Him."

1 JOHN 5:14-15 (NASB)

Look at the blessings of today
Giving thanks with a grateful heart,
Let God direct each step
Trust Him from the start.

"As you therefore have received Christ Jesus the Lord, so walk in Him, rooted and built up in Him and established in the faith, as you have been taught, abounding in it with thanksgiving."

COLOSSIANS 2:6-7 (NKJV)

"In everything give thanks; for this is God's will for you in Christ Jesus."

1 THESSALONIANS 5:18 (NASB)

God is your loving Father
Same yesterday, today, and tomorrow,
Throughout your day He's there
In joys, trials, and sorrow.

"Jesus Christ is the same yesterday
and today and forever."

HEBREWS 13:8 (NIV)

Every temptation that comes your way,
Every hardship that you endure,
Is a chance to show God's grace
He will reveal His power for sure.

"I can do all things through Him
who strengthens me."

PHILIPPIANS 4:13 (NASB)

Though the way is steep
When hardships come,
Cling tightly to God's hand
He'll walk you safely home.

"For I am the Lord, your God, who takes hold of your right hand and says to you, Do not fear; I will help you."

ISAIAH 41:13 (NIV)

"Come to Me, all who are weary and heavy-laden, and I will give you rest. Take My yoke upon you and learn from Me, for I am gentle and humble in heart, and you will find rest for your souls."

MATTHEW 11: 28-29 (NASB)

Through pain and suffering
In the treadmill of life,
Get alone with the Lord
So He can heal your strife.

"Although the Lord gives you the bread of adversity and the water of affliction, your teachers will be hidden no more; with your own eyes you will see them. Whether you turn to the right or to the left, your ears will hear a voice behind you, saying, 'This is the way; walk in it.'"

ISAIAH 30:20-21 (NIV)

Don't question God
Nor be dismayed,
Just trust in Him
He'll show the way.

God …
You give me a peace
As I put trust in You,
Maybe not what I planned
But You help me through.

God …
You work all things out
According to Your plan
Walking step-by-step
Always holding my hand.

"I am with you and will watch over you wherever you go, and I will bring you back to this land. I will not leave you until I have done what I have promised you."

GENESIS 28:15 (NIV)

If there's anyone who understands
It's the Lord whom you can trust,
His compassion is overwhelming
Leaning on Him is a must.

"Trust in the Lord with all your heart and
do not lean on your own understanding.
In all your ways acknowledge Him, and
He will make your paths straight."

PROVERBS 3:5-6 (NASB)

When you seek Jesus
There you'll find peace,
Take hold of His hand
And all worry will cease.

"God is our refuge and strength,
an ever-present help in trouble.
Therefore we will not fear, though
the earth give way and the mountains
fall into the heart of the sea."

PSALM 46:1-2 (NIV)

Trust the Lord
And seek His face,
He is there for you
No one can take His place.

"Seek the Lord and His strength; seek His face evermore!"

PSALM 105:4 (NKJV)

Adversity brings pain
God allows it for our good,
To help us trust Him more
To lean on Him as we should.

"Of Benjamin he said: 'The beloved of the Lord shall dwell in safety by Him, Who shelters him all the day long; and he shall dwell between His shoulders.'"

DEUTERONOMY 33:12 (NKJV)

Meet God alone each day
Let Him fill you with His peace,
As you rest in Him
Trust fully and believe.

"Whoever dwells in the shelter of the Most
High will rest in the shadow of the Almighty."

PSALM 91:1 (NIV)

Wisdom

In order to see God
Be quiet in your soul,
So your Master can whisper
His wisdom to behold.

"The beginning of wisdom is this: Get wisdom, and whatever you get, get insight."

PROVERBS 4:7 (ESV)

Lay aside every problem and worry
Each burden that weighs you down,
Fix your eyes on the race ahead
Run to win the Victor's Crown.

"Therefore, since we have so great a cloud of witnesses surrounding us, let us also lay aside every encumbrance and the sin which so easily entangles us, and let us run with endurance the race that is set before us, fixing our eyes on Jesus, the author and perfecter of faith, who for the joy set before Him endured the cross, despising the shame, and has sat down at the right hand of the throne of God."

HEBREWS 12:1-2 (NASB)

God keeps you in peace
When your mind stays on Him,
Anxious thoughts fade away
As His light shines within.

"You will keep him in perfect peace, whose mind is
stayed on You, because he trusts in You."

ISAIAH 26:3 (NKJV)

Sit still before God
Don't let worry get in the way,
Be calm and quiet
God will be with you today.

"For I am the Lord, your God who takes hold of your right hand and says to you, 'Do not fear; I will help you.'"

ISAIAH 41:13 (NIV)

"Cast all your anxiety on him because he cares for you."

1 PETER 5:7 (NIV)

It's easy to get weighed down
By problems surrounding your life,
As you look to God for strength
He overcomes all your strife.

"Though youths grow weary and tired, and vigorous young men stumble badly, yet those who wait for the Lord will gain new strength; they will mount up with wings like eagles, they will run and not get tired, they will walk and not become weary."

ISAIAH 40:30-31 (NASB)

Bring all your hopes and fears
Under God's mighty hand,
Through His love and peace
He will show you His plan.

"The plans of the heart belong to man, but the answer of the tongue is from the Lord."

PROVERBS 16:1 (ESV)

"Humble yourselves, therefore, under God's mighty hand, that he may lift you up in due time. Cast all your anxiety on him because he cares for you."

1 PETER 5:6-7 (NIV)

Worship

**Praise the name of Jesus
From whom all blessings flow,
The Maker of Heaven and earth
With infinite love He bestows.**

"Praise the Lord from the heavens;
praise him in the heights above.
Praise him, all his angels; praise him,
all his heavenly hosts."

PSALM 148:1-2 (NIV)

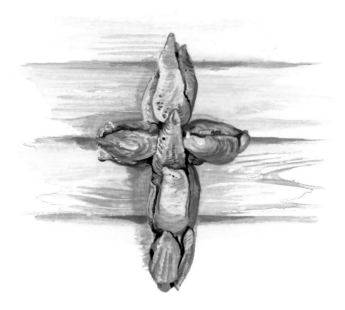

Worship is giving God your best
Of what He has given to you,
When you receive a blessing
Share it with others as a love gift, too.

"Worship the Lord with gladness; come before him with joyful songs .... Enter his gates with thanksgiving and his courts with praise; give thanks to him and praise his name. For the Lord is good and his love endures forever; his faithfulness continues through all generations."

PSALM 100:2, 4-5 (NIV)

As you lift up your hands
Praising the Lord above,
Let Him fill your heart
With joy, hope, and love.

"Shout joyfully to the Lord, all the earth; Break forth and sing for joy and sing praises."

PSALM 98:4 (NASB)